Life on the Fifth Floor

Guided Companion Journal

By: Dana Waters

JOURNAL FOR THE BOOK, LIFE ON THE FIFTH FLOOR:
THRIVING IN OUR 50S

Copyright © 2025 by Dana Waters. All rights reserved.
Published by Beyondthebookmedia.com

All rights reserved. No part of this publication may be reproduced, distributed, or transmitted in any form or by any means, including photocopying, recording, or other electronic or mechanical methods, without the prior written permission of the publisher, except in the case of brief quotations embodied in critical reviews and certain other noncommercial uses permitted by copyright law. For permission requests, write to the publisher, addressed "Attention: Permissions Coordinator," at the address below.

Limit of Liability/Disclaimer of Warranty: While the publisher and author have used their best efforts in preparing this book, they make no representations of warranties with respect to the accuracy or completeness of the contents of this book and specifically disclaim any implied warranties or merchantability or fitness for a particular purpose. No warranty may be created or extended by sales representatives or written sales materials. The advice and strategies contained herein may not be suitable for your situation. You should consult with a professional where appropriate. Neither the publisher nor author shall be liable for damages arising here from.

Beyond The Book Media, LLC
Alpharetta. GA
www.beyondthebookmedia.com

The publisher is not responsible for websites that are not owned by the publisher.

ISBN: 978-1-966430-01-8

Journaling: Establishing a habit of journaling offers many benefits that contribute to personal growth, emotional well-being, and cognitive development. Through consistent practice, individuals can harness the power of journaling to cultivate self-awareness, achieve goals, enhance creativity, and navigate life's challenges more effectively.

Writing: Writing in a daily journal promotes brain growth and cognitive function by stimulating neuroplasticity, improving memory, enhancing language skills, regulating emotions, fostering creativity, honing problem-solving abilities, and facilitating self-reflection. By incorporating journaling into our routine, we can harness these benefits to optimize brain health and cognitive performance.

Gratitude: Expressing gratitude offers many benefits for mental, emotional, and physical well-being. Regularly acknowledging and appreciating the good things in our lives cultivates a more positive mindset, strengthens relationships, reduces stress, and promotes happiness and fulfillment.

Affirming: affirming behaviors through journaling offers many benefits, including fostering positive self-talk, boosting self-confidence, setting intentions, cultivating gratitude, changing negative thought patterns, managing stress and anxiety, and enhancing self-acceptance. By incorporating affirmations into our journaling practice, we can promote personal growth, emotional well-being, and overall life satisfaction.

Repetition: Repetition is essential for forming habits. By consistently journaling affirmations, you're establishing a routine that reinforces positive thinking patterns. Over time, this habit can become ingrained, making it easier to maintain a positive mindset even outside our journaling sessions. It is a powerful tool for reprogramming our subconscious mind, cultivating a positive mindset, and fostering personal growth and development.

This Fifth Floor Journal Belongs To:

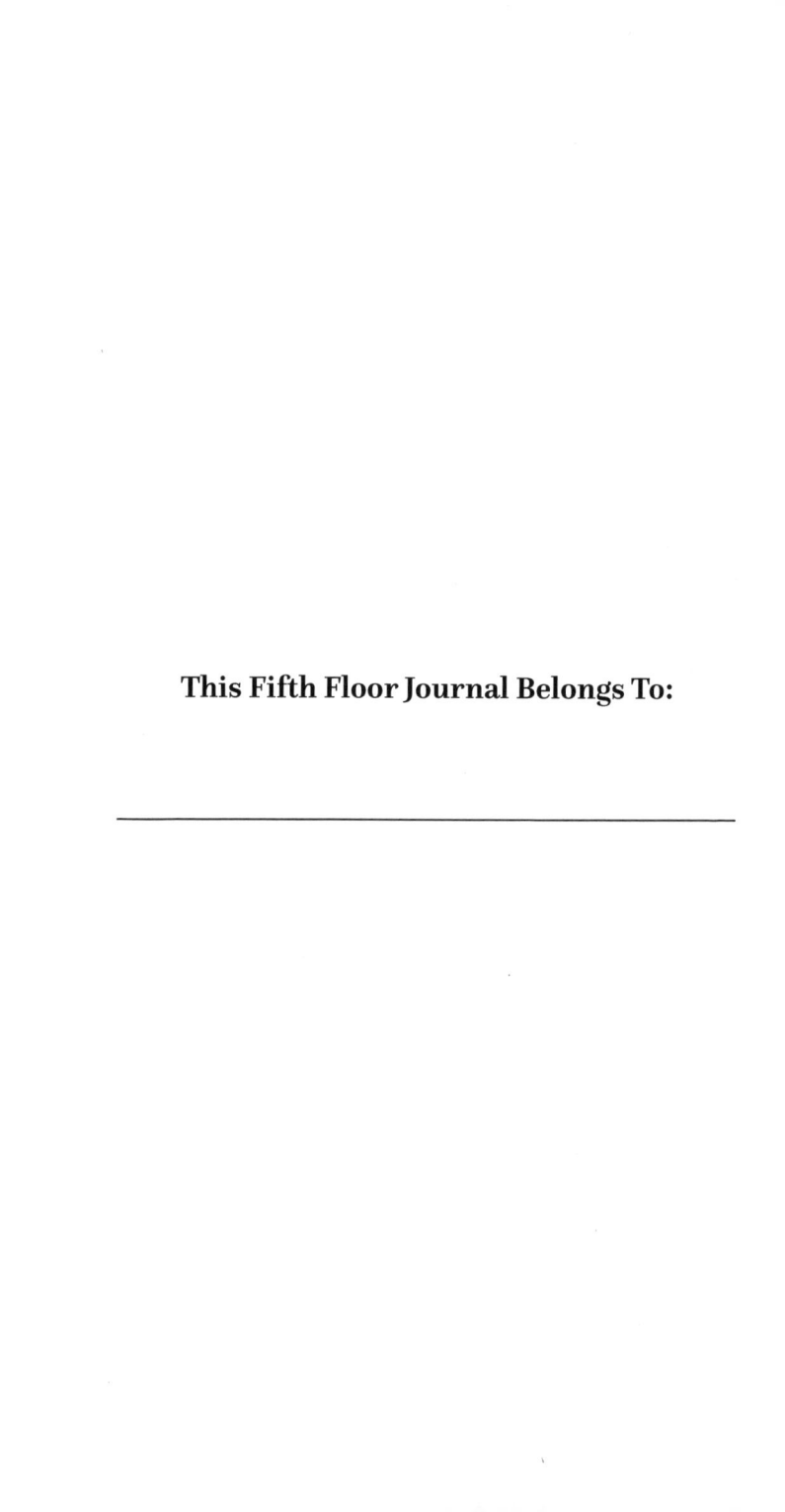

_____

Personal Commitment to Thrive on the Fifth Floor

I pledge on this day to commit wholeheartedly to thriving in Life on the Fifth Floor. I acknowledge that to truly thrive, I must be dedicated to my personal growth, and I promise to embark on this journey with purpose, intention, and self-compassion.

I vow to actively identify and map out my goals, ensuring that I not only set them but also strive to achieve them with persistence and clarity. I commit to navigating this transformative path with curiosity, resilience, and an open heart. I will write in my journal daily, using it as a tool for reflection, accountability, and progress, continuing until it is complete.

Throughout this journey, I promise to love, honor, and embrace myself fully, appreciating both the challenges and the victories. I will trust in my own power to evolve and flourish, knowing that this is a pivotal chapter of my life.

_____

Signature

_____

Start Date

_____

Completion Date

This is your Fifth Floor Life Goal Map and Journal.

You will use it to map out your fifth-floor goals, take inspired action daily, and align with the dreams and goals you establish for yourself in the fifth decade of this life.

Pay attention to your energy, be fluent, and trust yourself as you navigate the fifth floor and create the abundance, success, and life you desire

Let's Thrive!

How to Use the Daily Journal

Please write in this journal every day to express your gratitude, set intentions, communicate the actions you will take and how they align with the goals you set for yourself this year, and affirm yourself and your Fifth Floor Goals. Write your affirmations several times throughout the day or all at once. Use phrases as if you have already accomplished what you are affirming, like "I am," "I have," and "I am grateful that I am/I received/I completed." Be sure to reflect on the goals you set and your "why." If you feel you need more guidance, coaching, or accountability please visit
www.lifeonthefifthfloor.com
for additional resources.

How to Create Your Fifth Floor Life Goal Map:

Write your dreams, desires, and goals for this entire decade. It doesn't matter where you are in your 50s. List everything you would like to accomplish before you age out of this fifth decade of life. There is plenty of space for big dreamers, but don't worry about filling in every line. Your list should be specific to you, even if you feel they are out of reach.

Then, choose some of the goals from your list that you believe can be reasonably accomplished within the next five years. If you are further along in your 50s and don't have five years left in this decade, list out what you can accomplish in the years you have remaining in this decade.

Finally, write the goals you believe can be reasonably accomplished within one year.

The daily journal focus will be on your desires, goals, and dreams for this year.

Using this journal daily will take you through 90 days.

My Fifth Floor Goals:
What I would like to accomplish by the end of this decade of my life

(a comprehensive list of everything I would like to accomplish before the end of this decade)

My Fifth Floor Goals:
What I will accomplish within five years.

(goals from my "end of decade' list that I will accomplish within five years)

My Fifth Floor Goals:
What I will accomplish this year

(goals from my five-year list that I will pursue and accomplish this year)

A "why" statement is essential when setting goals because it provides clarity, purpose, and motivation. Creating a "why" statement involves deep reflection on your personal values, passions, and the underlying reasons behind your goals. Here's a step-by-step guide to help you develop a meaningful "why":

1. **Reflect on Your Values:** Start by identifying the core values that guide your life, such as family, growth, health, freedom, or creativity. Your "why" should align with these values, ensuring that it resonates deeply with who you are.

2. **Identify Your Passion:** Consider what excites or motivates you. What are the things you love to do or care about the most? Your "why" should be connected to something that inspires you and gives you energy.

3. **Think About Your Goals:** Look at the goals you want to achieve. Ask yourself why they matter to you. Why do you want to accomplish them? What difference will they make in your life or in the lives of others?

4. **Explore the Impact:** Consider how achieving your goals will benefit you and those around you. This impact is often the core of your "why" –it reflects the greater purpose behind your efforts.

5. **Keep It Simple and Authentic:** Your "why" statement doesn't need to be complicated. It should be clear, concise, and authentic. Aim to write a few sentences that capture the essence of your purpose and motivation.

6. **Test Its Strength:** Once you've written your "why," test it by asking if it truly inspires and drives you. It should feel compelling enough to push you through challenges and remind you of your bigger purpose.

My "Why" Statement:

_____
_____
_____
_____
_____

Date:_____

Today's word/intention/scripture...

_____

I am grateful for...

1. _____
2. _____
3. _____

The actions I am taking today that align with my Fifth Floor goals...

ACTION	GOAL
☐	
☐	
☐	
☐	
☐	
☐	
☐	
☐	
☐	
☐	
☐	
☐	
☐	
☐	
☐	
☐	
☐	

Affirm yourself and your Fifth Floor Goals.

Date:_____

Today's word/intention/scripture...

_____

I am grateful for...

1. _____
2. _____
3. _____

*The actions I am taking today that align with my
Fifth Floor goals...*

ACTION	GOAL
☐	
☐	
☐	
☐	
☐	
☐	
☐	
☐	
☐	
☐	
☐	
☐	
☐	
☐	
☐	
☐	
☐	

Affirm yourself and your Fifth Floor Goals.

Date:_____

Today's word/intention/scripture...

_____

I am grateful for...

1. _____
2. _____
3. _____

The actions I am taking today that align with my Fifth Floor goals...

ACTION	GOAL
☐	
☐	
☐	
☐	
☐	
☐	
☐	
☐	
☐	
☐	
☐	
☐	
☐	
☐	
☐	
☐	
☐	

Affirm yourself and your Fifth Floor Goals.

Date:_____

Today's word/intention/scripture...

I am grateful for...

1. _____
2. _____
3. _____

The actions I am taking today that align with my Fifth Floor goals...

ACTION	GOAL
☐	
☐	
☐	
☐	
☐	
☐	
☐	
☐	
☐	
☐	
☐	
☐	
☐	
☐	
☐	
☐	

Affirm yourself and your Fifth Floor Goals.

Date:_____

Today's word/intention/scripture...

I am grateful for...

1. _____
2. _____
3. _____

The actions I am taking today that align with my Fifth Floor goals...

ACTION	GOAL
☐	
☐	
☐	
☐	
☐	
☐	
☐	
☐	
☐	
☐	
☐	
☐	
☐	
☐	
☐	
☐	

Affirm yourself and your Fifth Floor Goals.

Date:_____

Today's word/intention/scripture...

_____

I am grateful for...

1. _____
2. _____
3. _____

The actions I am taking today that align with my Fifth Floor goals...

ACTION	GOAL
☐	
☐	
☐	
☐	
☐	
☐	
☐	
☐	
☐	
☐	
☐	
☐	
☐	
☐	
☐	
☐	

Affirm yourself and your Fifth Floor Goals.

Date:_____

Today's word/intention/scripture...

_____

I am grateful for...

1. _____
2. _____
3. _____

The actions I am taking today that align with my Fifth Floor goals...

ACTION	GOAL
☐	
☐	
☐	
☐	
☐	
☐	
☐	
☐	
☐	
☐	
☐	
☐	
☐	
☐	
☐	
☐	

Affirm yourself and your Fifth Floor Goals.

Date:_____

Today's word/intention/scripture...

_____

I am grateful for...

1. _____
2. _____
3. _____

The actions I am taking today that align with my Fifth Floor goals...

ACTION	GOAL
☐	
☐	
☐	
☐	
☐	
☐	
☐	
☐	
☐	
☐	
☐	
☐	
☐	
☐	
☐	
☐	

Affirm yourself and your Fifth Floor Goals.

Date:_____

Today's word/intention/scripture...

_____

I am grateful for...

1. _____
2. _____
3. _____

The actions I am taking today that align with my Fifth Floor goals...

ACTION	GOAL
☐	
☐	
☐	
☐	
☐	
☐	
☐	
☐	
☐	
☐	
☐	
☐	
☐	
☐	
☐	
☐	

Affirm yourself and your Fifth Floor Goals.

Date:_____

Today's word/intention/scripture...

I am grateful for...

1. _____
2. _____
3. _____

The actions I am taking today that align with my Fifth Floor goals...

ACTION	GOAL
☐	
☐	
☐	
☐	
☐	
☐	
☐	
☐	
☐	
☐	
☐	
☐	
☐	
☐	
☐	
☐	

Affirm yourself and your Fifth Floor Goals.

Date:_____

Today's word/intention/scripture...

_____

I am grateful for...

1. _____
2. _____
3. _____

The actions I am taking today that align with my Fifth Floor goals...

ACTION	GOAL
☐	
☐	
☐	
☐	
☐	
☐	
☐	
☐	
☐	
☐	
☐	
☐	
☐	
☐	
☐	
☐	
☐	

Affirm yourself and your Fifth Floor Goals.

Date:_____

Today's word/intention/scripture...

_____

I am grateful for...

1._____
2._____
3._____

*The actions I am taking today that align with my
Fifth Floor goals...*

ACTION	GOAL
☐	
☐	
☐	
☐	
☐	
☐	
☐	
☐	
☐	
☐	
☐	
☐	
☐	
☐	
☐	
☐	

Affirm yourself and your Fifth Floor Goals.

Date:_____

Today's word/intention/scripture...

_____

I am grateful for...

1. _____
2. _____
3. _____

The actions I am taking today that align with my Fifth Floor goals...

ACTION	GOAL
☐	
☐	
☐	
☐	
☐	
☐	
☐	
☐	
☐	
☐	
☐	
☐	
☐	
☐	
☐	
☐	
☐	

Affirm yourself and your Fifth Floor Goals.

Date:_____

Today's word/intention/scripture...

_____

I am grateful for...

1. _____
2. _____
3. _____

The actions I am taking today that align with my Fifth Floor goals...

ACTION	GOAL
☐	
☐	
☐	
☐	
☐	
☐	
☐	
☐	
☐	
☐	
☐	
☐	
☐	
☐	
☐	
☐	

Affirm yourself and your Fifth Floor Goals.

Date:_____

Today's word/intention/scripture...

_____

I am grateful for...

1. _____
2. _____
3. _____

The actions I am taking today that align with my Fifth Floor goals...

ACTION	GOAL
☐	
☐	
☐	
☐	
☐	
☐	
☐	
☐	
☐	
☐	
☐	
☐	
☐	
☐	
☐	
☐	

Affirm yourself and your Fifth Floor Goals.

Date:_____

Today's word/intention/scripture...

_____

I am grateful for...

1. _____
2. _____
3. _____

The actions I am taking today that align with my Fifth Floor goals...

ACTION	GOAL
☐	
☐	
☐	
☐	
☐	
☐	
☐	
☐	
☐	
☐	
☐	
☐	
☐	
☐	
☐	
☐	
☐	

Affirm yourself and your Fifth Floor Goals.

Date:_____

Today's word/intention/scripture...

_____

I am grateful for...

1. _____
2. _____
3. _____

The actions I am taking today that align with my Fifth Floor goals...

ACTION	GOAL
☐	
☐	
☐	
☐	
☐	
☐	
☐	
☐	
☐	
☐	
☐	
☐	
☐	
☐	
☐	
☐	

Affirm yourself and your Fifth Floor Goals.

Date:_____

Today's word/intention/scripture...

_____

I am grateful for...

1._____
2._____
3._____

The actions I am taking today that align with my Fifth Floor goals...

ACTION	GOAL
☐	
☐	
☐	
☐	
☐	
☐	
☐	
☐	
☐	
☐	
☐	
☐	
☐	
☐	
☐	
☐	

Affirm yourself and your Fifth Floor Goals.

Date:_____

Today's word/intention/scripture...

_____

I am grateful for...

1. _____
2. _____
3. _____

The actions I am taking today that align with my Fifth Floor goals...

ACTION	GOAL
☐	
☐	
☐	
☐	
☐	
☐	
☐	
☐	
☐	
☐	
☐	
☐	
☐	
☐	
☐	
☐	

Affirm yourself and your Fifth Floor Goals.

Date:_____

Today's word/intention/scripture...

_____

I am grateful for...

1. _____
2. _____
3. _____

The actions I am taking today that align with my Fifth Floor goals...

ACTION	GOAL
☐	
☐	
☐	
☐	
☐	
☐	
☐	
☐	
☐	
☐	
☐	
☐	
☐	
☐	
☐	
☐	

Affirm yourself and your Fifth Floor Goals.

Date:_____

Today's word/intention/scripture...

_____

I am grateful for...

1. _____
2. _____
3. _____

The actions I am taking today that align with my Fifth Floor goals...

ACTION	GOAL
☐	
☐	
☐	
☐	
☐	
☐	
☐	
☐	
☐	
☐	
☐	
☐	
☐	
☐	
☐	
☐	

Affirm yourself and your Fifth Floor Goals.

Date: _____

Today's word/intention/scripture...

_____

I am grateful for...

1. _____
2. _____
3. _____

The actions I am taking today that align with my Fifth Floor goals...

ACTION	GOAL
☐	
☐	
☐	
☐	
☐	
☐	
☐	
☐	
☐	
☐	
☐	
☐	
☐	
☐	
☐	
☐	
☐	

Affirm yourself and your Fifth Floor Goals.

Date:_____

Today's word/intention/scripture...

_____

I am grateful for...

1. _____
2. _____
3. _____

The actions I am taking today that align with my Fifth Floor goals...

ACTION	GOAL
☐	
☐	
☐	
☐	
☐	
☐	
☐	
☐	
☐	
☐	
☐	
☐	
☐	
☐	
☐	
☐	

Affirm yourself and your Fifth Floor Goals.

Date:_____

Today's word/intention/scripture...

_____

I am grateful for...

1. _____
2. _____
3. _____

The actions I am taking today that align with my Fifth Floor goals...

ACTION	GOAL
☐	
☐	
☐	
☐	
☐	
☐	
☐	
☐	
☐	
☐	
☐	
☐	
☐	
☐	
☐	
☐	

Affirm yourself and your Fifth Floor Goals.

Date:_____

Today's word/intention/scripture...

_____

I am grateful for...

1. _____
2. _____
3. _____

The actions I am taking today that align with my Fifth Floor goals...

ACTION	GOAL
☐	
☐	
☐	
☐	
☐	
☐	
☐	
☐	
☐	
☐	
☐	
☐	
☐	
☐	
☐	
☐	

Affirm yourself and your Fifth Floor Goals.

Date:_____

Today's word/intention/scripture...

_____

I am grateful for...

1. _____
2. _____
3. _____

The actions I am taking today that align with my Fifth Floor goals...

ACTION	GOAL
☐	
☐	
☐	
☐	
☐	
☐	
☐	
☐	
☐	
☐	
☐	
☐	
☐	
☐	
☐	
☐	
☐	

Affirm yourself and your Fifth Floor Goals.

Date:_____

Today's word/intention/scripture...

_____

I am grateful for...

1. _____
2. _____
3. _____

The actions I am taking today that align with my Fifth Floor goals...

ACTION	GOAL
☐	
☐	
☐	
☐	
☐	
☐	
☐	
☐	
☐	
☐	
☐	
☐	
☐	
☐	
☐	
☐	

Affirm yourself and your Fifth Floor Goals.

Date:_____

Today's word/intention/scripture...

_____

I am grateful for...

1. _____
2. _____
3. _____

The actions I am taking today that align with my Fifth Floor goals...

ACTION	GOAL
☐	
☐	
☐	
☐	
☐	
☐	
☐	
☐	
☐	
☐	
☐	
☐	
☐	
☐	
☐	
☐	

Affirm yourself and your Fifth Floor Goals.

Date:_____

Today's word/intention/scripture...

_____

I am grateful for...

1. _____
2. _____
3. _____

The actions I am taking today that align with my Fifth Floor goals...

ACTION	GOAL
☐	
☐	
☐	
☐	
☐	
☐	
☐	
☐	
☐	
☐	
☐	
☐	
☐	
☐	
☐	
☐	

Affirm yourself and your Fifth Floor Goals.

Date:_____

Today's word/intention/scripture...

_____

I am grateful for...

1. _____
2. _____
3. _____

The actions I am taking today that align with my Fifth Floor goals...

ACTION	GOAL
☐	
☐	
☐	
☐	
☐	
☐	
☐	
☐	
☐	
☐	
☐	
☐	
☐	
☐	
☐	
☐	
☐	

Affirm yourself and your Fifth Floor Goals.

Date:_____

Today's word/intention/scripture...

_____

I am grateful for...

1._____
2._____
3._____

*The actions I am taking today that align with my
Fifth Floor goals...*

ACTION	GOAL
☐	
☐	
☐	
☐	
☐	
☐	
☐	
☐	
☐	
☐	
☐	
☐	
☐	
☐	
☐	
☐	

Affirm yourself and your Fifth Floor Goals.

Date:_____

Today's word/intention/scripture...

_____

I am grateful for...

1. _____
2. _____
3. _____

The actions I am taking today that align with my Fifth Floor goals...

ACTION	GOAL
☐	
☐	
☐	
☐	
☐	
☐	
☐	
☐	
☐	
☐	
☐	
☐	
☐	
☐	
☐	
☐	

Affirm yourself and your Fifth Floor Goals.

Date:_____

Today's word/intention/scripture...

_____

I am grateful for...

1. _____
2. _____
3. _____

The actions I am taking today that align with my Fifth Floor goals...

ACTION	GOAL
☐	
☐	
☐	
☐	
☐	
☐	
☐	
☐	
☐	
☐	
☐	
☐	
☐	
☐	
☐	
☐	
☐	

Affirm yourself and your Fifth Floor Goals.

Date: _____

Today's word/intention/scripture...

_____

I am grateful for...

1. _____
2. _____
3. _____

The actions I am taking today that align with my Fifth Floor goals...

ACTION	GOAL
☐	
☐	
☐	
☐	
☐	
☐	
☐	
☐	
☐	
☐	
☐	
☐	
☐	
☐	
☐	
☐	

Affirm yourself and your Fifth Floor Goals.

Date:_____

Today's word/intention/scripture...

_____

I am grateful for...

1. _____
2. _____
3. _____

The actions I am taking today that align with my Fifth Floor goals...

ACTION	GOAL
☐	
☐	
☐	
☐	
☐	
☐	
☐	
☐	
☐	
☐	
☐	
☐	
☐	
☐	
☐	
☐	

Affirm yourself and your Fifth Floor Goals.

Date:_____

Today's word/intention/scripture...

_____

I am grateful for...

1. _____
2. _____
3. _____

The actions I am taking today that align with my Fifth Floor goals...

ACTION	GOAL
☐	
☐	
☐	
☐	
☐	
☐	
☐	
☐	
☐	
☐	
☐	
☐	
☐	
☐	
☐	
☐	

Affirm yourself and your Fifth Floor Goals.

Date:_____

Today's word/intention/scripture...

I am grateful for...

1. _____
2. _____
3. _____

The actions I am taking today that align with my Fifth Floor goals...

ACTION	GOAL
☐	
☐	
☐	
☐	
☐	
☐	
☐	
☐	
☐	
☐	
☐	
☐	
☐	
☐	
☐	
☐	

Affirm yourself and your Fifth Floor Goals.

Date:_____

Today's word/intention/scripture...

_____

I am grateful for...

1. _____
2. _____
3. _____

The actions I am taking today that align with my Fifth Floor goals...

ACTION	GOAL
☐	
☐	
☐	
☐	
☐	
☐	
☐	
☐	
☐	
☐	
☐	
☐	
☐	
☐	
☐	
☐	
☐	

Affirm yourself and your Fifth Floor Goals.

Date:_____

Today's word/intention/scripture...

_____

I am grateful for...

1. _____
2. _____
3. _____

The actions I am taking today that align with my Fifth Floor goals...

ACTION	GOAL
☐	
☐	
☐	
☐	
☐	
☐	
☐	
☐	
☐	
☐	
☐	
☐	
☐	
☐	
☐	
☐	

Affirm yourself and your Fifth Floor Goals.

Date:_____

Today's word/intention/scripture...

_____

I am grateful for...

1. _____
2. _____
3. _____

The actions I am taking today that align with my Fifth Floor goals...

ACTION	GOAL
☐	
☐	
☐	
☐	
☐	
☐	
☐	
☐	
☐	
☐	
☐	
☐	
☐	
☐	
☐	
☐	
☐	

Affirm yourself and your Fifth Floor Goals.

Date:_____

Today's word/intention/scripture...

_____

I am grateful for...

1. _____
2. _____
3. _____

The actions I am taking today that align with my Fifth Floor goals...

ACTION	GOAL
☐	
☐	
☐	
☐	
☐	
☐	
☐	
☐	
☐	
☐	
☐	
☐	
☐	
☐	
☐	
☐	

Affirm yourself and your Fifth Floor Goals.

Date:_____

Today's word/intention/scripture...

I am grateful for...

1. _____
2. _____
3. _____

*The actions I am taking today that align with my
Fifth Floor goals...*

ACTION	GOAL
☐	
☐	
☐	
☐	
☐	
☐	
☐	
☐	
☐	
☐	
☐	
☐	
☐	
☐	
☐	
☐	

Affirm yourself and your Fifth Floor Goals.

Date:_____

Today's word/intention/scripture...

_____

I am grateful for...

1. _____
2. _____
3. _____

The actions I am taking today that align with my Fifth Floor goals...

ACTION	GOAL
☐	
☐	
☐	
☐	
☐	
☐	
☐	
☐	
☐	
☐	
☐	
☐	
☐	
☐	
☐	
☐	
☐	

Affirm yourself and your Fifth Floor Goals.

Date:_____

Today's word/intention/scripture...

_____

I am grateful for...

1. _____
2. _____
3. _____

The actions I am taking today that align with my Fifth Floor goals...

ACTION	GOAL
☐	
☐	
☐	
☐	
☐	
☐	
☐	
☐	
☐	
☐	
☐	
☐	
☐	
☐	
☐	
☐	
☐	

Affirm yourself and your Fifth Floor Goals.

Date:_____

Today's word/intention/scripture...

_____

I am grateful for...

1._____
2._____
3._____

The actions I am taking today that align with my Fifth Floor goals...

ACTION	GOAL
☐	
☐	
☐	
☐	
☐	
☐	
☐	
☐	
☐	
☐	
☐	
☐	
☐	
☐	
☐	
☐	

Affirm yourself and your Fifth Floor Goals.

Date:_____

Today's word/intention/scripture...

_____

I am grateful for...

1. _____
2. _____
3. _____

The actions I am taking today that align with my Fifth Floor goals...

ACTION	GOAL
☐	
☐	
☐	
☐	
☐	
☐	
☐	
☐	
☐	
☐	
☐	
☐	
☐	
☐	
☐	
☐	

Affirm yourself and your Fifth Floor Goals.

Date:_____

Today's word/intention/scripture...

I am grateful for...

1. _____
2. _____
3. _____

The actions I am taking today that align with my Fifth Floor goals...

ACTION	GOAL
☐	
☐	
☐	
☐	
☐	
☐	
☐	
☐	
☐	
☐	
☐	
☐	
☐	
☐	
☐	
☐	
☐	

Affirm yourself and your Fifth Floor Goals.

Date:_____

Today's word/intention/scripture...

_____

I am grateful for...

1. _____
2. _____
3. _____

The actions I am taking today that align with my Fifth Floor goals...

ACTION	GOAL
☐	
☐	
☐	
☐	
☐	
☐	
☐	
☐	
☐	
☐	
☐	
☐	
☐	
☐	
☐	
☐	

Affirm yourself and your Fifth Floor Goals.

Date:_____

Today's word/intention/scripture...

I am grateful for...

1. _____
2. _____
3. _____

The actions I am taking today that align with my Fifth Floor goals...

ACTION	GOAL
☐	
☐	
☐	
☐	
☐	
☐	
☐	
☐	
☐	
☐	
☐	
☐	
☐	
☐	
☐	
☐	

Affirm yourself and your Fifth Floor Goals.

Date:_____

Today's word/intention/scripture...

_____

I am grateful for...

1._____
2._____
3._____

The actions I am taking today that align with my Fifth Floor goals...

ACTION	GOAL
☐	
☐	
☐	
☐	
☐	
☐	
☐	
☐	
☐	
☐	
☐	
☐	
☐	
☐	
☐	
☐	

Affirm yourself and your Fifth Floor Goals.

Date:_____

Today's word/intention/scripture...

_____

I am grateful for...

1. _____
2. _____
3. _____

The actions I am taking today that align with my Fifth Floor goals...

ACTION	GOAL
☐	
☐	
☐	
☐	
☐	
☐	
☐	
☐	
☐	
☐	
☐	
☐	
☐	
☐	
☐	
☐	
☐	

Affirm yourself and your Fifth Floor Goals.

Date:_____

Today's word/intention/scripture...

_____

I am grateful for...

1._____

2._____

3._____

The actions I am taking today that align with my
Fifth Floor goals...

ACTION	GOAL
☐	
☐	
☐	
☐	
☐	
☐	
☐	
☐	
☐	
☐	
☐	
☐	
☐	
☐	
☐	
☐	

Affirm yourself and your Fifth Floor Goals.

Date:_____

Today's word/intention/scripture...

_____

I am grateful for...

1. _____
2. _____
3. _____

*The actions I am taking today that align with my
Fifth Floor goals...*

ACTION	GOAL
☐	
☐	
☐	
☐	
☐	
☐	
☐	
☐	
☐	
☐	
☐	
☐	
☐	
☐	
☐	
☐	

Affirm yourself and your Fifth Floor Goals.

Date:_____

Today's word/intention/scripture...

_____

I am grateful for...

1. _____
2. _____
3. _____

*The actions I am taking today that align with my
Fifth Floor goals...*

ACTION	GOAL
☐	
☐	
☐	
☐	
☐	
☐	
☐	
☐	
☐	
☐	
☐	
☐	
☐	
☐	
☐	
☐	
☐	

Affirm yourself and your Fifth Floor Goals.

Date:_____

Today's word/intention/scripture...

_____

I am grateful for...

1. _____
2. _____
3. _____

The actions I am taking today that align with my Fifth Floor goals...

ACTION	GOAL
☐	
☐	
☐	
☐	
☐	
☐	
☐	
☐	
☐	
☐	
☐	
☐	
☐	
☐	
☐	
☐	

Affirm yourself and your Fifth Floor Goals.

Date:_____

Today's word/intention/scripture...

_____

I am grateful for...

1._____
2._____
3._____

The actions I am taking today that align with my Fifth Floor goals...

ACTION	GOAL
☐	
☐	
☐	
☐	
☐	
☐	
☐	
☐	
☐	
☐	
☐	
☐	
☐	
☐	
☐	
☐	

Affirm yourself and your Fifth Floor Goals.

Date:_____

Today's word/intention/scripture...

I am grateful for...

1. _____
2. _____
3. _____

The actions I am taking today that align with my Fifth Floor goals...

ACTION	GOAL
☐	
☐	
☐	
☐	
☐	
☐	
☐	
☐	
☐	
☐	
☐	
☐	
☐	
☐	
☐	
☐	

Affirm yourself and your Fifth Floor Goals.

Date:_____

Today's word/intention/scripture...

_____

I am grateful for...

1. _____
2. _____
3. _____

The actions I am taking today that align with my Fifth Floor goals...

ACTION	GOAL
☐	
☐	
☐	
☐	
☐	
☐	
☐	
☐	
☐	
☐	
☐	
☐	
☐	
☐	
☐	
☐	
☐	

Affirm yourself and your Fifth Floor Goals.

Date:_____

Today's word/intention/scripture...

_____

I am grateful for...

1. _____
2. _____
3. _____

The actions I am taking today that align with my Fifth Floor goals...

ACTION	GOAL
☐	
☐	
☐	
☐	
☐	
☐	
☐	
☐	
☐	
☐	
☐	
☐	
☐	
☐	
☐	
☐	
☐	

Affirm yourself and your Fifth Floor Goals.

Date:_____

Today's word/intention/scripture...

_____

I am grateful for...

1. _____
2. _____
3. _____

The actions I am taking today that align with my Fifth Floor goals...

ACTION	GOAL
☐	
☐	
☐	
☐	
☐	
☐	
☐	
☐	
☐	
☐	
☐	
☐	
☐	
☐	
☐	
☐	
☐	

Affirm yourself and your Fifth Floor Goals.

Date:_____

Today's word/intention/scripture...

_____

I am grateful for...

1._____
2._____
3._____

The actions I am taking today that align with my Fifth Floor goals...

ACTION	GOAL
☐	
☐	
☐	
☐	
☐	
☐	
☐	
☐	
☐	
☐	
☐	
☐	
☐	
☐	
☐	
☐	

Affirm yourself and your Fifth Floor Goals.

Date: _____

Today's word/intention/scripture...

_____

I am grateful for...

1. _____
2. _____
3. _____

The actions I am taking today that align with my Fifth Floor goals...

ACTION	GOAL
☐	
☐	
☐	
☐	
☐	
☐	
☐	
☐	
☐	
☐	
☐	
☐	
☐	
☐	
☐	
☐	

Affirm yourself and your Fifth Floor Goals.

Date:_____

Today's word/intention/scripture...

_____

I am grateful for...

1._____
2._____
3._____

The actions I am taking today that align with my Fifth Floor goals...

ACTION	GOAL
☐	
☐	
☐	
☐	
☐	
☐	
☐	
☐	
☐	
☐	
☐	
☐	
☐	
☐	
☐	
☐	

Affirm yourself and your Fifth Floor Goals.

Date:_____

Today's word/intention/scripture...

_____

I am grateful for...

1. _____
2. _____
3. _____

The actions I am taking today that align with my Fifth Floor goals...

ACTION	GOAL
☐	
☐	
☐	
☐	
☐	
☐	
☐	
☐	
☐	
☐	
☐	
☐	
☐	
☐	
☐	
☐	

Affirm yourself and your Fifth Floor Goals.

Date:_____

Today's word/intention/scripture...

_____

I am grateful for...

1._____
2._____
3._____

The actions I am taking today that align with my Fifth Floor goals...

ACTION	GOAL
☐	
☐	
☐	
☐	
☐	
☐	
☐	
☐	
☐	
☐	
☐	
☐	
☐	
☐	
☐	
☐	
☐	

Affirm yourself and your Fifth Floor Goals.

Date:_____

Today's word/intention/scripture...

_____

I am grateful for...

1. _____
2. _____
3. _____

*The actions I am taking today that align with my
Fifth Floor goals...*

ACTION	GOAL
☐	
☐	
☐	
☐	
☐	
☐	
☐	
☐	
☐	
☐	
☐	
☐	
☐	
☐	
☐	
☐	

Affirm yourself and your Fifth Floor Goals.

Date:_____

Today's word/intention/scripture...

_____

I am grateful for...

1._____
2._____
3._____

The actions I am taking today that align with my Fifth Floor goals...

ACTION	GOAL
☐	
☐	
☐	
☐	
☐	
☐	
☐	
☐	
☐	
☐	
☐	
☐	
☐	
☐	
☐	
☐	

Affirm yourself and your Fifth Floor Goals.

Date:_____

Today's word/intention/scripture...

_____

I am grateful for...

1. _____
2. _____
3. _____

The actions I am taking today that align with my Fifth Floor goals...

ACTION	GOAL
☐	
☐	
☐	
☐	
☐	
☐	
☐	
☐	
☐	
☐	
☐	
☐	
☐	
☐	
☐	
☐	

Affirm yourself and your Fifth Floor Goals.

Date:_____

Today's word/intention/scripture...

_____

I am grateful for...

1. _____
2. _____
3. _____

The actions I am taking today that align with my Fifth Floor goals...

ACTION	GOAL
☐	
☐	
☐	
☐	
☐	
☐	
☐	
☐	
☐	
☐	
☐	
☐	
☐	
☐	
☐	
☐	

Affirm yourself and your Fifth Floor Goals.

Date:_____

Today's word/intention/scripture...

_____

I am grateful for...

1. _____
2. _____
3. _____

The actions I am taking today that align with my Fifth Floor goals...

ACTION	GOAL
☐	
☐	
☐	
☐	
☐	
☐	
☐	
☐	
☐	
☐	
☐	
☐	
☐	
☐	
☐	
☐	

Affirm yourself and your Fifth Floor Goals.

Date:_____

Today's word/intention/scripture...

_____

I am grateful for...

1._____
2._____
3._____

*The actions I am taking today that align with my
Fifth Floor goals...*

ACTION	GOAL
☐	
☐	
☐	
☐	
☐	
☐	
☐	
☐	
☐	
☐	
☐	
☐	
☐	
☐	
☐	
☐	

Affirm yourself and your Fifth Floor Goals.

Date:_____

Today's word/intention/scripture...

I am grateful for...

1. _____
2. _____
3. _____

The actions I am taking today that align with my Fifth Floor goals...

ACTION	GOAL
☐	
☐	
☐	
☐	
☐	
☐	
☐	
☐	
☐	
☐	
☐	
☐	
☐	
☐	
☐	
☐	

Affirm yourself and your Fifth Floor Goals.

Date:_____

Today's word/intention/scripture...

_____

I am grateful for...

1._____
2._____
3._____

*The actions I am taking today that align with my
Fifth Floor goals...*

ACTION	GOAL
☐	
☐	
☐	
☐	
☐	
☐	
☐	
☐	
☐	
☐	
☐	
☐	
☐	
☐	
☐	
☐	
☐	

Affirm yourself and your Fifth Floor Goals.

Date:_____

Today's word/intention/scripture...

_____

I am grateful for...

1. _____
2. _____
3. _____

The actions I am taking today that align with my Fifth Floor goals...

ACTION	GOAL
☐	
☐	
☐	
☐	
☐	
☐	
☐	
☐	
☐	
☐	
☐	
☐	
☐	
☐	
☐	
☐	

Affirm yourself and your Fifth Floor Goals.

Date:_____

Today's word/intention/scripture...

I am grateful for...

1. _____
2. _____
3. _____

The actions I am taking today that align with my Fifth Floor goals...

ACTION	GOAL
☐	
☐	
☐	
☐	
☐	
☐	
☐	
☐	
☐	
☐	
☐	
☐	
☐	
☐	
☐	
☐	

Affirm yourself and your Fifth Floor Goals.

Date:_____

Today's word/intention/scripture...

_____

I am grateful for...

1. _____
2. _____
3. _____

The actions I am taking today that align with my Fifth Floor goals...

ACTION	GOAL
☐	
☐	
☐	
☐	
☐	
☐	
☐	
☐	
☐	
☐	
☐	
☐	
☐	
☐	
☐	
☐	
☐	

Affirm yourself and your Fifth Floor Goals.

Date:_____

Today's word/intention/scripture...

_____

I am grateful for...

1. _____
2. _____
3. _____

The actions I am taking today that align with my Fifth Floor goals...

ACTION	GOAL
☐	
☐	
☐	
☐	
☐	
☐	
☐	
☐	
☐	
☐	
☐	
☐	
☐	
☐	
☐	
☐	
☐	

Affirm yourself and your Fifth Floor Goals.

Date:_____

Today's word/intention/scripture...

_____

I am grateful for...

1. _____
2. _____
3. _____

The actions I am taking today that align with my Fifth Floor goals...

ACTION	GOAL
☐	
☐	
☐	
☐	
☐	
☐	
☐	
☐	
☐	
☐	
☐	
☐	
☐	
☐	
☐	
☐	
☐	

Affirm yourself and your Fifth Floor Goals.

Date:_____

Today's word/intention/scripture...

_____

I am grateful for...

1. _____
2. _____
3. _____

The actions I am taking today that align with my Fifth Floor goals...

ACTION	GOAL
☐	
☐	
☐	
☐	
☐	
☐	
☐	
☐	
☐	
☐	
☐	
☐	
☐	
☐	
☐	
☐	
☐	

Affirm yourself and your Fifth Floor Goals.

Date:_____

Today's word/intention/scripture...

_____

I am grateful for...

1._____
2._____
3._____

The actions I am taking today that align with my Fifth Floor goals...

ACTION	GOAL
☐	
☐	
☐	
☐	
☐	
☐	
☐	
☐	
☐	
☐	
☐	
☐	
☐	
☐	
☐	
☐	
☐	

Affirm yourself and your Fifth Floor Goals.

Date:_____

Today's word/intention/scripture...

_____

I am grateful for...

1._____
2._____
3._____

The actions I am taking today that align with my Fifth Floor goals...

ACTION	GOAL
☐	
☐	
☐	
☐	
☐	
☐	
☐	
☐	
☐	
☐	
☐	
☐	
☐	
☐	
☐	
☐	
☐	

Affirm yourself and your Fifth Floor Goals.

Date:_____

Today's word/intention/scripture...

I am grateful for...

1. _____
2. _____
3. _____

The actions I am taking today that align with my Fifth Floor goals...

ACTION	GOAL
☐	
☐	
☐	
☐	
☐	
☐	
☐	
☐	
☐	
☐	
☐	
☐	
☐	
☐	
☐	
☐	

Affirm yourself and your Fifth Floor Goals.

Date:_____

Today's word/intention/scripture...

I am grateful for...

1. _____
2. _____
3. _____

The actions I am taking today that align with my Fifth Floor goals...

ACTION	GOAL
☐	
☐	
☐	
☐	
☐	
☐	
☐	
☐	
☐	
☐	
☐	
☐	
☐	
☐	
☐	
☐	
☐	

Affirm yourself and your Fifth Floor Goals.

You're Almost There!

Congratulations on making it this far! As you approach the final days of this journal, it's the perfect time to think ahead and ensure your journey continues. Reorder your next companion journal today to keep up the momentum. Visit Amazon to purchase your next journal and stay on track with your personal growth and reflection.

Need Extra Support?

If you're looking for additional guidance to help you achieve your goals, consider signing up for personalized coaching. Whether you want to dive deeper into your journey or stay accountable, I'm here to help. Visit ***www.lifeonthefifthfloor.com*** to learn more and sign up for coaching today.

Date:_____

Today's word/intention/scripture...

_____

I am grateful for...

1._____
2._____
3._____

*The actions I am taking today that align with my
Fifth Floor goals...*

ACTION	GOAL
☐	
☐	
☐	
☐	
☐	
☐	
☐	
☐	
☐	
☐	
☐	
☐	
☐	
☐	
☐	
☐	
☐	

Affirm yourself and your Fifth Floor Goals.

Date:_____

Today's word/intention/scripture...

_____

I am grateful for...

1._____
2._____
3._____

The actions I am taking today that align with my Fifth Floor goals...

ACTION	GOAL
☐	
☐	
☐	
☐	
☐	
☐	
☐	
☐	
☐	
☐	
☐	
☐	
☐	
☐	
☐	
☐	

Affirm yourself and your Fifth Floor Goals.

Date:_____

Today's word/intention/scripture...

_____

I am grateful for...

1. _____
2. _____
3. _____

The actions I am taking today that align with my Fifth Floor goals...

ACTION	GOAL
☐	
☐	
☐	
☐	
☐	
☐	
☐	
☐	
☐	
☐	
☐	
☐	
☐	
☐	
☐	
☐	

Affirm yourself and your Fifth Floor Goals.

Date:_____

Today's word/intention/scripture...

_____

I am grateful for...

1._____
2._____
3._____

The actions I am taking today that align with my Fifth Floor goals...

ACTION	GOAL
☐	
☐	
☐	
☐	
☐	
☐	
☐	
☐	
☐	
☐	
☐	
☐	
☐	
☐	
☐	
☐	
☐	

Affirm yourself and your Fifth Floor Goals.

Date:_____

Today's word/intention/scripture...

_____

I am grateful for...

1. _____
2. _____
3. _____

The actions I am taking today that align with my Fifth Floor goals...

ACTION	GOAL
☐	
☐	
☐	
☐	
☐	
☐	
☐	
☐	
☐	
☐	
☐	
☐	
☐	
☐	
☐	
☐	
☐	

Affirm yourself and your Fifth Floor Goals.

Date:_____

Today's word/intention/scripture...

_____

I am grateful for...

1. _____
2. _____
3. _____

The actions I am taking today that align with my Fifth Floor goals...

ACTION	GOAL
☐	
☐	
☐	
☐	
☐	
☐	
☐	
☐	
☐	
☐	
☐	
☐	
☐	
☐	
☐	
☐	
☐	

Affirm yourself and your Fifth Floor Goals.

Date:_____

Today's word/intention/scripture...

_____

I am grateful for...

1._____
2._____
3._____

*The actions I am taking today that align with my
Fifth Floor goals...*

ACTION	GOAL
☐	
☐	
☐	
☐	
☐	
☐	
☐	
☐	
☐	
☐	
☐	
☐	
☐	
☐	
☐	
☐	
☐	

Affirm yourself and your Fifth Floor Goals.

Made in the USA
Columbia, SC
07 May 2025